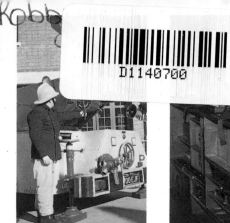

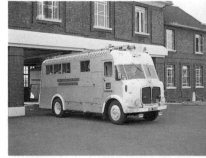

We quite often see a fire engine racing through the streets of our towns or cities but did you know that firemen do much more than just putting out fires? This book, written simply for young children and illustrated with over one hundred full-colour photographs, looks behind the scenes at the day-to-day work of the fire service.

Acknowledgments

The author and publishers would like to thank the following for their help, support and co-operation during the production of this book: Leicestershire Fire Service; Hampshire Fire Brigade for the photographs on pages 5, 6, 7, 8, 9, 38 and 50; and Jack Stretton for the photographs on pages 4, 28 (top) and 33.

First Edition

© LADYBIRD BOOKS LTD MCMLXXXII

People who help us
THE FIRE SERVICE

written by IRENE DODDS

photographs by TIM CLARK

Ladybird Books Loughborough

When you see a fire engine racing along the road, do you ever wonder about the firemen and the work they do? They have a very important job.

4

Whenever there is a fire, the firemen must put it out as quickly as they can. If people are in danger, the firemen have to rescue them and take them to safety.

Fighting fires is the firemen's main job, but they help people in many other ways as well.

Firemen use heavy cutters to cut away wreckage after motor vehicle accidents

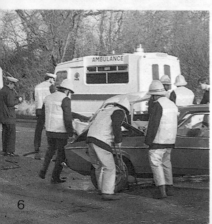

When there is a car crash, or a train goes off the rails, people can be trapped in the wreckage.

The firemen can cut them free or get them out if they are trapped under something heavy.

Often someone gets stuck on a roof or falls down a steep cliff.

Firemen wearing chemical splash suits and breathing apparatus to remove dangerous chemicals ·

The firemen can use their ropes and ladders to rescue them.

After heavy rain there may be flooding. If a house or a shop is flooded the firemen use their pumps to get rid of the water.

Long ladders are not only used to reach rooftops and high windows. Firemen need to be very inventive in the use of their equipment, as in the rubbish dump fire below

Sometimes dangerous chemicals are spilt by accident. Then the firemen go with their hoses and wash them away before anyone can be hurt.

Washing away any dangerous chemicals after a damaged container has been removed

They may make a dam with soil or sand to stop chemicals getting into drains. Then they can be taken away safely.

Firemen are trained to do all sorts of different jobs.

The place where they work and keep all their equipment is called a *fire station*. Every large town and city has at least one fire station.

In each station there is an *appliance room* where the fire engines are kept.

This room has large doors which usually lead on to the street. When these doors are opened, they go up out of the way so that the fire engines can get out quickly.

Some appliance room doors are automatic. The ones in the pictures are raised by hand

The Land Rover pump carries 100 gallons (455 litres) of water and is used in tight spaces to get closer to a fire

At a large station there are three or
four fire engines, which the firemen
call *fire appliances*. Each appliance
has a different job to do.

The *water tender ladder* is very useful. It carries a ladder about 14 metres long, and holds 400 gallons (1818 litres) of water. This water can be used if there is no other water supply near the fire.

Above: *The back of the crew cab showing breathing apparatus situated so that it can be put on while the appliance is driving to the fire*

Left: *The side locker in an appliance contains about 80 different items of equipment*

The appliance with the longest ladder is called a *turntable ladder*. This ladder is about 30 metres long. It is used when there is a fire in a high building, and it can be turned in any direction.

With this ladder a fireman can send a

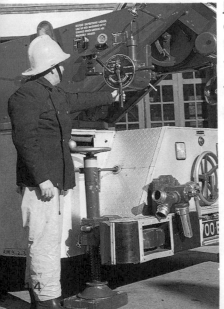

jet of water down on to the roof of a burning building. When it is used in this way, the ladder is called a *water tower*. The same ladder is often used to rescue people.

A fireman operates the turntable ladder. When the ladder has been extended it can be moved to the left or right

Some stations also have a *hydraulic platform* or *snorkel*. This appliance has a long extending arm divided into sections. It can be moved and set over buildings at different angles.

The snorkel provides a safe working platform and can get further in over a fire. It is used as a water tower and for rescue

There is a long pipe running up the arm of the snorkel. This can carry a large flow of water and gives a strong jet to use on the fire.

The platform houses a giant tap, called a monitor, which is trained in the direction of the fire

Another important appliance is the *emergency tender*, which carries a lot of tools and equipment.

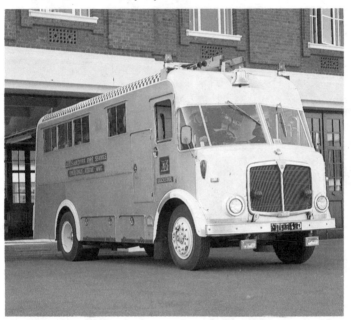

The firemen mainly use this appliance when they are called out to accidents.

The emergency tender carries extra breathing apparatus, communications equipment, protective clothing and many other items including First Aid

17

Firemen must be ready to fight fires and to help people at all times of the day and night.

Firemen take daily exercise in the form of volley ball

To make sure of this the firemen at each station are divided into *watches*. There are four watches. Each one has the name of a colour. Usually they are called *red watch*, *white watch*, *green watch* and *blue watch*.

Every fireman belongs to one of these watches. Each time a fireman finishes his work, another fireman from a different watch comes in and takes over his place. In this way the station always has enough firemen on duty. In small villages part-time firemen may do other jobs until a bleeper in their pocket tells them there is a fire.

The first thing a fireman does when

he starts work is to look at the *duty board*. This tells him which appliance to go on if there is a fire or some other call for help.

They have their meals and can play games at the fire station

He then goes to that appliance and puts all his fire-fighting clothes in his own place. He has a long navy-blue tunic, a yellow helmet, yellow waterproof trousers, and a pair of boots.

If there is a fire or other emergency he will have to get dressed in a hurry while on the way. So he sets out his clothes in a special way. His tunic and helmet may be hung on a peg.

Beside them go his waterproof trousers and his fire boots. The trousers are carefully folded down over the boots so that they can be pulled up quickly. Some firemen leave their uniform ready in the fire appliance.

At a fire the fireman's clothes are
very important to him. They help to
keep him dry and also safe from
harm.

To keep dry, he wears the waterproof trousers and fire boots. The trousers are bright yellow to make it easier to see him when there is thick smoke at the fire.

The boots keep his feet dry. They have extra-strong toecaps in case something heavy falls on his feet.

Fire boots are specially made and have special soles which stop dangerous chemicals soaking through

His helmet is yellow too. It is made from hard cork covered with fabric. This strong helmet helps to protect the fireman's head from sharp or heavy objects falling from above.

A fireman also uses an axe. Axes are hung inside the appliance. As he gets dressed, the fireman takes an axe and fits it into a sling fixed to his tunic. At a fire he mainly uses his axe to chop away burning wood.

Look at the clothing worn by different members of the fire service

1 Senior Divisional Officer (left) and a Station Officer

2 A Firewoman. A large number of women work in the fire service as administrators but many also attend fires to provide food, drinks and extra transport for the firefighters

3 Fireman in working overalls

4 Fireman in full fire kit

5 A chemical splash suit which has a double lining at the cuffs and ankles

6 A gas-tight suit which is a one-piece suit, including the boots and mask, and is used especially where chemicals are giving off dangerous fumes

6

4

5

How do firemen know when there is a fire?

When someone spots a fire, they hurry to the nearest telephone. There they dial the number 999.

If you dial 999 and ask for the fire brigade, your call is put through to the county fire brigade control room, who then connect you to your nearest fire station

The telephone operator answers this call right away. Then the operator puts it through to the central control room and from there to the nearest fire station.

An officer checks the map to find the nearest available fire appliance

When a chemical has been spilled, its name is fed to the computer which shows what action needs to be taken to prevent damage and further danger

At once a loud alarm signal is set
off at this fire station. This can be
heard all over the station.

When the firemen hear this noise, they
stop what they are doing. Quickly they
run to the appliance room.

If they are upstairs, often they slide down a polished pole. This runs through an opening in the ceiling and leads down to the appliance room. It is quicker to use this pole than to run down flights of stairs.

While they are doing this, central control will tell them over a loudspeaker where the fire is.

Sliding down the highly polished pole to the appliance room

There are five men in the crew of each appliance. One fireman is the driver. He jumps into the cab and starts the engine. The other firemen get into the back.

While this is happening, the big doors of the appliance room have been opened. The fire appliances drive out and race to the fire. As they go, they sound their sirens. This loud noise warns the traffic ahead that they are coming.

One fireman is always in charge of all the others. This officer has usually been in the Fire Brigade for many years.

A leading fireman (left) *and a sub officer* (right) *with a station officer. His white helmet with its black cone makes him easily seen by his men at a fire*

The sub officer in charge of the appliance

He sits beside the driver of the
leading machine. He keeps in touch
with the control room by radio and
makes sure that they are going to the
right address.

When they reach the fire, the firemen look for the nearest *fire hydrant*. This is marked with the letter **H** on a yellow metal plate.

Hydrants are regularly cleaned and tested

Under the ground there is a large pipe, called a water main, which brings water to our homes. The numbers on the hydrant plate tell the firemen the size of the water main and how

far this is from the hydrant.
The firemen can get water from the
water main by fixing on a *stand-pipe*.

The stand-pipe raises the water
above ground level. The firemen
connect their hoses to the stand-pipe
and this gives them all the water they
need to fight the fire.

This shows a hose attached to the stand-pipe and ready for use

When it is a big fire, several appliances are needed. The firemen use lots of hoses, sending water onto the fire from all directions, until it is out.

If the fire is in the country, the firemen look for the nearest pond or stream. Then they use the appliance to siphon the water out of the pond and pump it through their hoses.

After the fire is out, the firemen go back to the fire station. There they take the wet hoses, wash them and hang them up inside a tall tower to dry.

All the equipment is checked. Clean, dry hoses are put on each appliance. Everything must be ready in case there is another fire.

Washing the hoses

Clean, dry hoses ready for re-use

Even when there are no fires the firemen are still busy. The fire station usually has a big yard where they can practise all the skills they need to fight fires and handle other emergencies.

Running out the hose from an appliance, to test it

Re-filling the breathing apparatus cylinders with compressed air

There they also test their ladders and pumps. They check the hoses to make sure that they do not leak. All their equipment must be in good order.

Patching a hose

43

Sometimes they practise going into buildings filled with smoke. It is difficult to breathe in thick smoke, so the firemen have to wear *breathing apparatus*.

This is a piece of equipment worn on the fireman's back. It has a face mask joined to a supply of air, and helps the fireman to breathe properly.

A fireman in full fire-fighting kit. Breathing apparatus is used at most big fires because so many modern materials used to make furniture for example, give off dangerous fumes when they are on fire

When he goes into smoke-filled buildings, he often carries a *two-way radio* as well. This keeps him in touch with the other firemen outside.

Before a fireman enters a building he gives his tally to the breathing apparatus control officer. This has the fireman's name on it and is attached to a board which shows what time he went in, how much air he has and the time he should come out of the building

A fireman must learn how to deal with all kinds of fires. Some fires cannot be put out by using water. They have to be smothered with a special kind of *foam*.

A high expansion foam generator

The appliance which carries this is called a *foam tender*.

The generator sucks in water which mixes with detergent and is blown out as foam by a large fan

Washing away excess foam after the fire has been put out

A special chemical unit goes to all accidents or incidents involving dangerous chemicals. When the chemicals have been made safe or taken away, a special *decontamination* area is set up for the firemen.

A fireman in his gas-tight suit hands his tally to the breathing apparatus control officer

Each man is washed, fully clothed, before he is allowed to leave the area. Then he strips off his clothes and takes a shower in the mobile unit, to make sure that no harmful chemicals are left on his body.

In hot, dry weather there are sometimes grass fires. For these the firemen use special beaters made of canvas or old hose, as well as water.

Often fires begin because someone has been careless. In our own homes, fires can start with things like chip pans or electric blankets. Cigarette ends, too, are dangerous.

The firemen like to give people advice on how to avoid having a fire. This work is called *fire prevention*.

A factory Health and Safety officer discusses fire prevention with a fireman

They go to places such as hotels, shops, schools and factories, and look for things which might start fires. They make sure there are *fire doors* and *fire exits*. Nowadays firemen spend a lot of time doing this kind of work, for they think it is very important.